Tobias Picker
b.1954

ARIAS

for Soprano and Piano

Edited by
Samuel Bill
Juan Pablo Contreras
Scott Wollschleger

ED 30122

www.schott-music.com

Mainz · London · Madrid · New York · Paris · Prague · Tokyo · Toronto
© 2014 SCHOTT HELICON MUSIC CORPORATION, New York · Printed in USA

Contents

Foreword

When it comes to American opera, we are living in the middle of a Renaissance — or a boom, if you will, since the intensity of creative activity devoted to composing and producing new operas has no real precedent in this country. Tobias Picker has been a major part of this Renaissance over the past two decades, from the moment he launched his career as an opera composer with *Emmeline* at Santa Fe Opera.

It's far from usual, with one's first attempt at this complex, interdependent, hybrid genre, to hit the kind of home run Mr. Picker achieved. Yet he had wisely taken his time before embarking on *Emmeline*. A creative prodigy, Mr. Picker spent the first decades of his career developing a distinctive voice in his orchestral, chamber, and solo compositions — and honing compositional skills that have informed every aspect of his writing for the stage.

It wasn't until he'd reached the age of 40 that creative urge and circumstance converged in a commission to set Judith Rossner's novel about Emmeline Mosher, a fictionalized account of a real-life nineteenth-century woman and her grimly tragic fate. But since then Mr. Picker has produced a catalogue of five substantial operas — not to mention chamber versions of several of these to enable performances by smaller companies and a major new revision of *An American Tragedy* for its revival at the 2014 Glimmerglass Festival.

Because so much of his subject matter centers on the passions and emotional turmoil of ordinary people caught up in realistic, unforgiving situations, Mr. Picker's operatic style was soon branded "American verismo." As far as such comparisons go, he says he doesn't mind, even finding this a compliment, though it says nothing about his music itself — beyond the fact that each of his operas is seamlessly structured to allow for the heightened moments of revelation to which arias and varied ensembles are so well suited.

By collaborating with such gifted librettists as the poet J.D. McClatchy and Gene Scheer, Mr. Picker ensures that these numbers enhance and give dimension to his characters — from Clyde Griffiths consumed by blinding ambition to grab his piece of the American dream and Thérèse Raquin's guilt-haunted conscience after the murder of her husband to Dolores Claiborne's moving attempt to explain her choices to her hardened daughter. "The words are another color for me," says Mr. Picker, whose settings take detailed account of the natural rhythms of language, thus bringing to mind another comparison that J.D. McClatchy has suggested: Janáček who similarly crafted indelible portraits of strong women "in a claustrophobic society."

Despite the unique sound world Mr. Picker constructs for each of these operas, they circle around recurrent shared themes: the struggle against repressive conventions, the situation of powerless but determined women, the illusion of religious consolation. Even the plot devices and settings of the literary sources on which he has drawn — from Theodore Dreiser and Emile Zola to Stephen King — contain uncanny echoes in their climactic scenes of drowning or trial. *Fantastic Mr. Fox*, based on the children's story by Roald Dahl, is an exception in being a comedy — but here, too, the comedy has a dark, sardonic edge, and the singing animals also serve an allegorical function as social commentary.

Yet for all the melodramatic, even Gothic, situations of his narratives, Mr. Picker's musical characterizations paint astute psychological portraits. Aria after aria in this collection shows him using the tools of his trade and the expressive power of the human voice to reveal a character's inner life or sense of self in the face of extreme situations. He might call for dramatic leaps in range to underscore Roberta Alden's desperation intensifying; or the high-lying vocal line of the murdered husband Camille come back as a ghost; or a sweet, resigned lyricism to depict lovesickness in "Miss Hedgehog's Aria" from *Fantastic Mr. Fox*. "Opera is about telling stories in music," emphasizes Mr. Picker. That's true not only across the large canvas of an entire opera but within the limits of an aria as well. For this composer, arias become a narrative microcosm and a key to character. As such, they call for skills both musical and dramatic from their interpreters, but the challenges posed by these pieces will give corresponding pleasure.

Thomas May
Author of *Decoding Wagner*
2014

About the Operas

Emmeline
(1996)
An opera in two acts
Libretto by J.D. McClatchy
Based on the novel by Judith Rossner
Commissioned by Santa Fe Opera

World Premiere: July 27, 1996: Santa Fe Opera
George Manahan, conductor
Francesca Zambello, director

Premiere Cast:
Emmeline Mosher: Patricia Racette (soprano)
Matthew Gurney: Curt Peterson (tenor)
Mr. Maguire: Victor Ledbetter (baritone)
Aunt Hannah Watkins: Anne-Marie Owens (dramatic contralto)
Henry Mosher: Kevin Langan (bass)
Sophie: Melanie Sarakatsannis (soprano)
Pastor Avery: Herbert Perry (bass)
Mrs. Bass: Josepha Gayer (mezzo-soprano)

Synopsis of *Emmeline*
by J.D. McClatchy

In mid-century rural Maine, 13-year-old Emmeline Mosher, the eldest child of a poor farming family, is sent to work at a textile mill. She is soon seduced by her married supervisor, becomes pregnant, and is dismissed from her job. Her aunt arranges to have the child—which Emmeline never sees—adopted. Twenty years later, back at home to care for her elderly parents, Emmeline falls in love with and marries a mysterious young stranger, Matthew Gurney. When her aunt comes to visit, it is revealed that Matthew is, in fact, her stolen child. Unable to bear the thought of losing both a husband and a son, Emmeline begs Matthew to stay, but he abandons her, disgusted. Emmeline is subsequently condemned and ostracized by the townspeople, but she bravely refuses to yield to others and resolves to stay put, triumphing in her very survival.

Based on a true story—and, more broadly, an Oedipal framework from Jocasta's point of view—*Emmeline* makes a heroine out of the unfortunate woman, reimagining events so that her inner life is given a moral shape. She is a powerful figure who seeks to free herself from the oppressive circumstances of the society she is part of—a society that denied women their share of passion and power, and demanded that religion control their actions. Picker's vivid, precisely orchestrated score proceeds deftly, never letting a scene outlast its welcome. The object of international acclaim, *Emmeline* is recognized as one of America's most important and successful operas of the second half of the twentieth century.

Fantastic Mr. Fox
(1998)
An opera in three acts
Libretto by Donald Sturrock
Based on the book by Roald Dahl
Originally commissioned to benefit the Roald Dahl Foundation (now Roald Dahl's Marvellous Children's Charity) with funding from Felicity Dahl.

World Premiere:
December 9, 1998; Los Angeles Opera
Peter Ash, conductor
Donald Sturrock, director

Premiere Cast:
Mr. Fox: Gerald Finley (baritone)
Mrs. Fox: Suzanna Guzmán (mezzo-soprano)
Farmer Boggis: Louis Lebherz (bass)
Farmer Bunce: Doug Jones (tenor)
Farmer Bean: Jamie Offenbach (bass-baritone)
Mavis the Tractor: Lesley Leighton (soprano)
Agnes the Digger: Jill Grove (mezzo-soprano)
Miss Hedgehog: Sari Gruber (soprano)
Badger the Miner: Malcolm MacKenzie (baritone)
Burrowing Mole: Jorge Garza (tenor)
Rita the Rat: Josepha Gayer (mezzo-soprano)
Porcupine: Charles Castronovo (tenor)

Synopsis of *Fantastic Mr. Fox*
by Donald Sturrock

Mr. Fox is the darling of the animals in the forest. He is clever, debonair and never at a loss for schemes to feed both family and friends. But he has enemies, and this time he may have met his match. A sinister trio of grotesque farmers, led by the evil Farmer Bean, will stop at nothing in their plans to destroy him and his family. The story of how the Foxes and their friends survive the farmers and their mechanical allies, Mavis the Tractor and Agnes the Digger, is a stirring one, yet it is one that is also filled with unexpected humour and edgy wit.

Based on one of the most popular stories of the celebrated children's author, Roald Dahl, *Fantastic Mr. Fox* is a tuneful, rhythmic work whose music is by turns funny, sad and frightening. Although Dahl's story is for children, Picker's opera operates at multiple levels of meaning, also serving as a modern fable about oppression and the struggles between good and evil and between mankind and nature. Since its premiere it has been revived in many new productions in the UK and USA, enchanting audiences of adults and children alike with its madcap energy and zany humor. Encompassing a variety of playful, catchy musical elements, including a love duet between a hedgehog and a porcupine as well as an unconventional fox-trot for the Foxes, the opera is guaranteed to appeal to anyone still youthful at heart.

Thérèse Raquin
(2001)
An opera in two acts
Libretto by Gene Scheer
Based on the novel by Émile Zola
Commissioned by The Dallas Opera, L'Opéra de Montréal and
The San Diego Opera

World Premiere:
November 30, 2001; Dallas Opera
Graeme Jenkins, conductor
Francesca Zambello, director

Premiere Cast:
Madame Lisette Raquin: Diana Soviero (soprano)
Thérèse Raquin: Sara Fulgoni (mezzo-soprano)
Camille Raquin: Gordon Gietz (tenor)
Laurent: Richard Bernstein (baritone)
Suzanne Michaud: Sheryl Woods (soprano)
Olivier Michaud: Gagor Andrasy (bass)
Monsieur Grivet: Peter Kazaras (tenor)

Synopsis of *Thérèse Raquin*
by Gene Scheer

Married Parisian couple Thérèse and Camille Raquin are reunited with an old friend, Laurent. It soon becomes clear that Thérèse and Laurent are more than old friends. Their intense passion stands in strong contrast to the loveless marriage that Camille and Therese have been enduring. Desperate to find a way of being together, Therese and Laurent conspire to drown Camille in the Seine. After the crime is committed the guilty couple begins a tragic descent, as they are tormented by their own consciences and the ghost of Camille.

For the plot to Picker's second opera, we have his sister, Ida Picker, to thank: she introduced Emile Zola's 1867 novel *Thérèse Raquin* to her brother after an old copy of the book fell off her bookshelf while dusting. The resulting opera proceeds with remarkable intensity, heightening the drama with its suspenseful and highly rhythmic score. Its music hovers between tonality and complex atonality, with the latter taking on a stronger role in the second act, as Thérèse and Laurent come to grips with their crime. Picker masterfully creates an intricate web of counterpoint via acrobatic vocal lines.

An American Tragedy
(2005)
Opera in Two Acts
Libretto by Gene Scheer
Based on the novel by Theodore Dreiser
Commissioned by The Metropolitan Opera

World Premiere:
December 2, 2005; The Metropolitan Opera
James Conlon, conductor
Francesca Zambello, director

Premiere Cast:
Roberta Alden: Patricia Racette (soprano)
Sondra Finchley: Susan Graham (mezzo-soprano)
Clyde Griffiths: Nathan Gunn (baritone)
Elvira Griffiths: Dolora Zajick (mezzo-soprano)
Elizabeth Griffiths: Jennifer Larmore (mezzo-soprano)
Samuel Griffiths: Kim Begley (tenor)
Gilbert Griffiths: William Burden (tenor)
Orville Mason: Richard Bernstein (baritone)
Hortense: Anna Christy (soprano)

Synopsis of *An American Tragedy*
by Gene Scheer

Clyde Griffiths, a poor, Midwestern missionary's 20-year-old son takes a job in his affluent uncle's factory in upstate New York. Clyde soon rises to the position of foreman and is warned of a no fraternization policy between management and staff. Despite this warning, Clyde pursues a factory worker named Roberta Alden. As this relationship is developing, Clyde is introduced to the socialite world of his uncle's children. After spending a night with Roberta, Clyde begins a romantic relationship with Sondra Finchley, the beautiful daughter of one of the town's industrialists. When Clyde plans to break off the relationship with Roberta to pursue this new romance, he discovers that Roberta is pregnant. Clyde schemes to rid himself of his unwanted lover with a child on the way.

An adaptation of Theodore Dreiser's novel by the same name, *An American Tragedy* is a progressive drama of temptation, responsibility, and faith that ponders a common dilemma at the heart of the American experience: in this land of hope and boundless promise, how do we find the balance between our moral duties and our quest for the American dream? These questions live in the space between every note of Picker's powerfully meticulous work, and while searching for their answers, he has spun them into melodies that capture the optimism, sorrow and frailty of Clyde Griffith's "Everyman."

Dolores Claiborne
(2013)
An opera in two acts
Libretto by J.D. McClatchy
Based on the novel by Stephen King
Commissioned by San Francisco Opera

World Premiere:
September 18, 2013; San Francisco, CA
George Manahan, conductor
James Robinson, director

Premiere Cast:
Dolores Claiborne: Patricia Racette (soprano) / Catherine Cook (mezzo-soprano)
Vera Donovan: Elizabeth Futral (soprano)
Joe St. George: Wayne Tigges (bass-baritone)
Selena St. George: Susannah Biller (soprano)
Detective Thibodeau: Greg Fedderly (tenor)

Synopsis of *Dolores Claiborne*
by J.D. McClatchy

The opera opens with an interrogation, police officers accusing Dolores Claiborne of murdering the rich and imperious Vera Donovan, who employed Dolores as a maid and companion for forty years. As Dolores answers the officers' questions, we learn how her difficult marriage ended in the murder of her depraved husband, who had been sexually molesting their teen-age daughter. It is then revealed that Vera and Dolores were close friends, and that Vera left her entire fortune to Dolores. Even after learning of her innocence in Vera's death, Dolores's emotionally fraught daughter cannot forgive her mother—and even though Dolores has done everything a mother and woman can to keep three lives together, ultimately she is left alone.

Based on the best-selling novel by Stephen King, *Dolores Claiborne* is one of the most compelling characters to emerge from the esteemed writer's imagination. Passionate, desperate, trapped, the feisty Maine house-keeper will do anything to save the daughter who despises her. Dolores is a natural fit for opera—specifically for Picker's dark theatricality. *Dolores Claiborne* is Picker's fifth opera, a musical and dramatic triumph.

About the Arias

Emmeline

Letter Aria
Character: Emmeline
Setting: Mrs. Bass' boarding house, Lowell, Massachusetts (1841)
Emmeline is writing home. She is interrupted by Mr. Maguire, who is calling her name from beneath her window. Excited but confused, she decides, "It's easier just to obey."

Maryanne Aria
Character: Emmeline
Setting: The Mosher family home, Fayette, Maine (1861)
Emmeline pours her heart out to her mute and demented mother. Frustrated by Aunt Hannah's refusal to provide information, Emmeline chooses to believe she gave birth to a daughter twenty years earlier. Emmeline names her imaginary daughter Maryanne.

Everything I Want Is Gone
Character: Emmeline
Setting: Emmeline and Matthew's home, Fayette, Maine (1861)
After learning the truth from Aunt Hannah, Matthew has left for good. Shunned by all, Emmeline longs for Matthew and looks back on her tragic life.

Fantastic Mr. Fox

Miss Hedgehog's Aria
Character: Miss Hedgehog
Setting: The Fox family den
Miss Hedgehog, a lonely spinster, comes to call on Mrs. Fox and bemoans her fate of endless loneliness.

An American Tragedy

You Have To Marry Me, Clyde
Character: Roberta Alden
Setting: Roberta Alden's apartment, a poor section of Lycurgus, New York
Roberta tells the two-timing Clyde he has made her pregnant and that he must therefore marry her. Angry, she suspects he is no longer interested in her because she is poor.

Letter Aria
Character: Roberta Alden
Setting: The farm near Utica, New York where she grew up
With rising impatience, the pregnant Roberta writes Clyde a letter. She implores him to save her from the unthinkable disgrace of having a child out of wedlock.

Dolores Claiborne

Accidents Can Be An Unhappy Woman's Best Friend
Character: Vera Donovan
Setting: Vera Donavan's summer estate on Little Tall Island off the coast of Maine (1963)
Vera has just learned that her servant Dolores is married to a wife beater and child molester. She explains to Dolores that husbands die every day. Vera hints that she arranged for her unfaithful husband to meet with "an accident." This gives Dolores the idea to murder her husband Joe during the upcoming solar eclipse by making it look like an accident.

The Years Slip By
Character: Vera Donovan
Setting: Vera's bedroom in her summer estate on Little Tall Island off the coast of Maine (1963)
Old and frail, Vera Donovan sings to Dolores of the emptiness and tedium of her life as a bed-ridden woman.

There Should Not Be Stars
Character: Selena Saint George
Setting: Under the stars during the solar eclipse (1963)
Unaware that her mother Dolores has just murdered her father Joe Saint George, Selena is amazed at seeing stars in the middle of the day and wishes that this one happy moment would last forever.

Letter Aria
from "Emmeline"

J.D. McClatchy

Tobias Picker

There is lit-tle news here in Lowell. Mis-sus Bass is a com-fort. God tru-ly shows His grace to those who la-bor in His cause. One girl has sent home thir-ty dol-lars. I miss you___ all. Lov-ing re-gard to you, and to my dear broth-ers and sis-ters, Luke, An-drew, Har-riet, El-len, Sa-rah, Han-nah, Lit-tle Hen-ry,___ and the

It's eas-i-er just to o-bey.

Molto tranquillo

What am I to an-swer? What does he want me to say?

(MAGUIRE:)

Em - me - line. Em - me - line.

Maryanne
from "Emmeline"

J.D. McClatchy

Tobias Picker

Who would pro-tect___ me?___ Who could for-give?__ You___ nev-er told me men and

wom-en have the pow-er to ru-in one an-oth-er, to drag___ the life___

___ out of each oth-er, to cause___ such___ pain.___ All this

si-lence, all this shame.___

Everything I Want Is Gone
from "Emmeline"

J.D. McClatchy

Tobias Picker

ED 30122

Mat - thew!

Miss Hedgehog's Aria
from "Fantastic Mr. Fox"

Donald Sturrock

Tobias Picker

ED 30122

never a - gain feel the surge of warm blood rise in my

bod - y and quick - en my spir - it. Yes, time's hoar-y fin-ger en-

ti - ces me clos - er and clos - er and clos - er and then,

then I know sol-i-tude is my friend.

You Have To Marry Me, Clyde

from "An American Tragedy"

Gene Scheer

Tobias Picker

ED 30122

Letter Aria
from "An American Tragedy"

Gene Scheer

Tobias Picker

saved me the thrash - ing I de - served.   Ma - ma's made me a fine new silk - en

rall.   a tempo

dress.   But ev - 'ry   time____ it's fit - ted   I

break down.   I'm so fright - ened.____   I   don't care

where you go,   what you're do - ing,   who you've been with.   Just come____ for me soon.__ Don't leave me here. I can't lie to poor dear Ma-ma an-y-

more. Please think of all I had to give up. The sum - mer's

pleas-ure has__ been lost_____ wait-ing for you.

My dear Clyde, I can - not wait for - ev - er. Not__ for-ev - er.__

You must come for me. Take me a - way. Heav-en bless you.

Accidents Can Be An Unhappy Woman's Best Friend
from "Dolores Claiborne"

J.D. McClatchy

Tobias Picker

The Years Slip By
from "Dolores Claiborne"

J.D. McClatchy

Tobias Picker

There Should Not Be Stars
from "Dolores Claiborne"

J.D. McClatchy

Tobias Picker

Then the moon stole the sun.

The stars won - dered what had been done.

They're s'posed to wait, on - ly shine when it's late.

Some - thing's not right. Why is to - day to - night?

There___ should_____ not,_____ there should not be stars.___

___There should not be stars on just___ an - y___ old day._____

There___ should not___ be___ stars._____

But how I love them up there.

Noth - ing but stars eve - ry - where.

Just like can - dles in a mer-maid's cas - tle,

the sil - ver light caught in her hair.

But all of that was a mo - ment a - go,

so long a - go, it was just an-oth - er day.

There should not be stars on just an - y old day,

there___ should_____ not be stars.__ There should not,

but I nev - er want_ them___ to_____ go___ a - - - way.

I___ nev - - - -

- - er, nev - er, nev - er, nev - er want, nev - er, nev - er, nev - er, nev - er, nev - er want

them to_____ go___

a - way._____